Practical Mental Influence

Practical Mental Influence
By William Walker Atkinson

Wilder Publications, LLC.
PO Box 3005
Radford VA 24143-3005

ISBN 10: 1-60459-052-1
ISBN 13: 978-1-60459-052-4

First Edition

10 9 8 7 6 5 4 3 2 1

A Course of Lessons on
Mental Vibrations, Psychic Influence, Personal Magnetism,
Fascination, Psychic Self-Protection, etc., etc.

.

Containing
Practical Instruction, Exercises, Directions, etc.,
capable of being understood, mastered and demonstrated
by any person of average intelligence.

.

Table of Contents

THE LAW OF VIBRATION

Students of history find a continuous chain of reference to the mysterious influence of one human mind over that of others. In the earliest records, traditions and legends may be found giving reference to the general belief that it was possible for an individual to exert some weird uncanny power over the minds of other persons, which would influence the latter for good or evil. And more than this, the student will find an accompanying belief that certain individuals are possessed of some mental power which bends even "things" and circumstances to its might.

Way back in the dim past of man's history on this planet, this belief existed, and it has steadily persisted in spite of the strenuous opposition of material science, even unto the present day. The years have not affected the belief, and in these dawning days of the Twentieth Century it has taken on a new strength and vitality, for its adherents have boldly stepped to the front, and confronting the doubting materialistic thinkers, have claimed the name of "Science" for this truth and have insisted that it be taken, once and for all, from the category of superstition, credulity and ignorant phantasm.

Were it not pitiable, it would be amusing to glance at the presumptuous, complacent, smug, self-satisfied position of the materialistic school of thinkers, who would brush aside as a foolish delusion that which many of the wisest men of a past age have accepted and taught as the truth. The modern "know-it-alls" would sneer contemptuously at facts that are known to be of actual occurrence in the daily lives of thousands of intelligent people, and which the experience of humankind has demonstrated for many centuries, in all lands and all races.

The trouble lies in the dogmatic assumption of the materialistic school that what is known as "mind" is merely some peculiar action of the material brain, some writers even holding that "the brain secretes thought, just as the liver secretes bile." They refuse to see that the operation of Mind is a manifestation of energy known as electricity, magnetism, light, heat, gravitation, cohesion, etc. Because mental energy does not register the vibrations of these lower forms of energy, they conclude that the higher mental energy does not exist. Having formulated a theory to suit their materialistic conceptions, they try to ignore all facts not consistent with their theory. If they find a fact that will not squeeze into their narrow theory well, "so much the worse for the fact," as a writer has said and they promptly ignore or dispute it.

As a matter of truth, the investigator is not compelled to resort to metaphysical explanations to account for the phenomena of Mental Influence. The very facts of physical science itself, if rightly interpreted, will give the clue to the mystery; and will point the steps of the honest investigator toward the path where he may find the solution of the perplexing riddle. Although we know that the real solution lies in the metaphysical realm, still even physical science will corroborate the facts of its metaphysical sister science, and instead of contradicting the latter will actually go far toward furnishing analogous facts and principles basis for a theory of metaphysical facts.

The student will see at once that so far as physical science is concerned, it must begin at the phenomenon of "Thought Transference," for in that phase of the subject may be found an elementary principle in evidence in many other forms of phenomena. We have given many instances of "Thought Transference" in the two proceeding volumes of this series, entitled "Mind Reading" and "Psychomancy," respectively, and so we need not repeat the same in this place. The main fact is that "Thought Transference" does exist, and may be accounted for upon purely scientific grounds, without calling in the truths of metaphysical thought. We know that this is a strong statement, and a positive assertion, but we also know that the same may be demonstrated. Let us consider this phase of the subject.

In the first place, physical science teaches that underlying all forms, degrees and apparent differences in matter and energy, there is to be found a manifestation of some elementary energy, which manifests in what is known as "Vibrations." Everything in the material world is in vibration — ever manifesting a high degree of motion. Without vibration there would be no such thing as a material universe. From the electronic-corpuscles which science teaches compose the atom; up through the atom and molecule, until the most complex forms of matter are manifested, there is the ever-present Vibration. And through all forms of energy, light, heat, electricity, magnetism and the rest, Vibration is also ever present. In fact, physical science itself teaches that not only is Vibration the basic force underlying other forces and the various forms of matter, but also that the apparent differences between the various forms of matter, and also between the various forms of energy, are caused simply and solely by the varying degrees of Vibration manifested.

Just as the difference between the lowest tone that can be distinguished by the ear of man, and the highest note that can be distinguished by the same organ of sense, is merely a difference between the rate of Vibration — just as is the difference between the dull red color at one end of the spectrum, and the violet at the other end, with the intervening colors known as indigo, blue green, yellow and orange, with all the combinations of shades arising from them — just as the difference between the greatest degree of cold known to Science, and the greatest degree of heat that can be conceived of — just as these great differences due solely and wholly to varying rates of Vibration — so is the difference between and all forms of matter or force simply a matter of the rate of Vibration. In short, all material and physical "Things" are simply manifestations of some "infinite and eternal energy from which all things proceed," their differences resulting merely from the different degree of Vibration being manifested in them. Remember, that this is not "vague philosophy" or "airy metaphysics" or "spiritualistic vagaries" (to quote from the materialistic writers), but facts claimed and admitted by the greatest physical scientists of the age, as a reference to their lectures and textbooks will prove to anyone.

And, more than this, any intelligent physical scientist will tell you that Science has every reason to believe that there are great fields of energy and force, the Vibrations of which are far too high for even the delicate instruments of science to record, but which nevertheless exist and manifest effects. It was only the other day that Science was able to "catch" the "X-rays" and other forms of high Radioactivity, and yet these rays and forces had always existed. And tomorrow Science will perfect instruments capable of registering still higher forms of energy. And bye-and-bye, some scientist will perfect an instrument capable of registering and recording the subtle vibrations of Thought, and perhaps in time someone will perfect that instrument so that it will not only record such Thought vibrations and waves, but, like the phonograph, it will be able to reproduce and send forth similar vibrations so that others may feel the thoughts, just as they now hear the sounds from the phonograph. Such a prediction is no more wonderful then would have been the prediction of the telephone, the phonograph, the wireless telegraph and sundry other discoveries and inventions a hundred years ago.

Did you ever think that there are colors that the eye cannot see, but which delicate instruments clearly register? In fact, the rays of tight which sunburn the face, and which register on the photographic plate are not visible to the eye. The eye sees the lower rays, but only instruments adapted for the purpose detect the higher ones. Your eye cannot see the X-ray as it passes through the room, but the plate will catch it, and its light may make a photograph. The rays of light visible to the eyes are only the lower ones — the higher ones are far beyond the power of the eye to record, and beyond even the range of the most delicate instrument there exist rays and waves of light of such high vibratory rate as to defy even its power to record.

Did you ever know that there are sounds unheard by human ears that the microphone will catch and magnify? Scientific imagination dreams of instruments that will catch the songs of the mite — like insects, and magnify them until they can be distinguished. There are waves of electricity that may pass through your body, unperceived by you, and yet powerful enough to run light electric lights. Listen to the words of certain eminent scientists.

Prof. Elisha Gary, a celebrated scientist and teacher, has said: "There is much food for speculation in the thought that there exists sound waves that no human ear can hear, and color waves of light that no eye can see. The long, dark, soundless space between 40, 000 and 400,000,000,000,000 vibrations per second, and the infinity of range beyond 700,000,000,000,000 vibrations per second, where light ceases, in the universe of motion, makes it possible to indulge in speculation."

Prof. Williams, the well-known scientific writer, has said: "There is no gradation between the most rapid undulations or trembling that produces our sensations of sound, and the slowest of those which give rise to our sensations of gentlest warmth. There is a huge gap between them, wide enough to include another world of motion, all lying between our world of sound and our world of heat and light; and there is no good reason whatever for supposing that matter is incapable of such intermediate activity, or that such activity may not give rise to intermediate sensations, provided that there are organs for taking up and sensitizing their movements."

And, so you see that in the scientific theory of Vibrations, there may be found plenty of room for a scientific explanation of all that is claimed by adherents of the truth of Mental Influence, without getting out of the region of physical science, and without invading the plane of metaphysics. And there are many more proofs from the same source, which we may touch upon as we proceed.

There is but one Truth, and it manifests on all planes — the Spiritual; the Mental; and the Physical — and manifestations agree and coincide. So no Mentalist need fear the test of Physical Science, for each plane will bear out the facts and phenomena of the ones below or above it — the Three are but varying phases of One. In this little work we shall hug close to the plane of Physical Science, because by so doing we will be able to make the subject much clearer to many than if we had attempted to express the teaching in Metaphysical terms. There is no contradiction in the end. Each bit of Truth must dovetail into every other bit, for all are parts of the Whole.

Thought Waves

In our last chapter we have seen that Vibration was to be found underlying all manifestations of energy, and all forms of matter. We also quoted two distinguished scientists whose words showed that there were fields of vibratory energy not filled by any known forms of energy, the inference being that inasmuch as there are no gaps in nature's processes these unknown fields must be occupied by certain forms of energy not known as yet to physical science. The teachings of the occultists of all lands and ages, as also those of modern Mental Science, are to the effect that the Mind, in its manifestation of Thought in the brain, generates a form of energy of intensely high Vibration, which energy may be, and is, projected in vibratory waves from the brains of other persons within its field of influence.

All students of Mental Influence have noticed the close resemblance that is manifested between the phenomena of electrical and magnetic energy on the one hand and the phenomena of mental energy on the other. So close is the analogy that one may take the proven facts of science relating to electrical and magnetic phenomena and confidently proceed with the certainty of finding a strikingly close correspondence in the field of mental phenomena. And the recognition of this fact is helping the workers in the mental field group together the varied phenomena that come under their notice, and to work out the theory and practice of Mental Influence.

In the first place, it is now a fact well known and accepted by investigators that the generation of Thought and the manifestation of Mental States occasions a "burning up" of brain matter, and the consequent production of a form of energy of high vibratory power. Physiologists recognize this fact, and the textbooks make reference to it. Experiments have shown that the temperature of the brain is increased in accordance with the intensity of Feeling and Thought, and that there is undoubtedly a generation of energy and a consumption of brain matter which bears a very close resemblance to the process of the generation of electrical energy.

And this being conceded, it follows that this energy once released must be emanated or sent forth from the brain in the manner akin to the emanation of other known forms of energy, i.e., in the form of "waves" of vibratory force. Light and Heat travel in this way — so do electricity and magnetism — so do the forces of Radioactivity. And the investigators of Mental Influence have demonstrated by their experiments that there is such a thing as Thought-induction, and many other phases of manifestation similar to that exhibited by electricity and magnetism.

Flammarion, the well-known and eminent French scientist, has said on the subject. "We sum up, therefore, our preceding observations by the conclusion that one mind can act at a distance upon another, without the habitual medium of words, or any other visible means of communication. It appears to us altogether unreasonable to reject this conclusion if we accept the facts. The conclusion will be abundantly demonstrated. There is nothing unscientific, nothing romantic in admitting that an idea can influence a brain from a distance. The action of one human being upon another, from a distance, is a scientific fact, it is as certain as the existence of Paris, of Napoleon, of Oxygen, or of Sirius." The same authority also states: "There can be no doubt that our physical force creates a movement in the either which transmits itself afar like all movements in the ether, becomes perceptible to brains in harmony with our own. The transformation of a psychic action into an ethereal movement, and the reverse, may be analogous to what takes place on a telephone, where the receptive plate, which is identical with the plate at the other end, reconstructs the sonorous movement transmitted, not by means of sound, but by electricity. But these are only comparisons."

When a Thought or feeling is generated in the mind or brain of a person, the energy generated flows forth from the brain of the person in the form of waves of mental energy, spreading from the immediate neighborhood of the thinker to a distance proportioned to the strength of the thought or feeling. These Thought-Waves have the property of awakening similar vibrations in the minds of other persons coming within their field of force, according to the laws of Mental Influence, which law shall be explained in the next chapter.

As we proceed with our consideration of the subject of Mental Influence, in the succeeding chapters, we shall see the many and varied forms of manifestation of Thought-Waves. At this point we shall merely view the phenomena in a general way.

Thought-Waves are manifested in a variety of forms and phases. Some are the waves emanated from the minds of all thinkers, unconsciously and without purpose, and usually without much force. Others are sent forth with great force, and travel far, manifesting a degree of influence commensurate with the force with which they are projected. Others are directed purposely toward certain individuals or places, and travel along rapidly in a straight line to the point which they have been directed or aimed. Others are sent forth with great strength and power, but instead of being directed toward any particular person or place, are designed to sweep around in great whirlpools of energy affecting all who happen to fall within their field force.

You will readily understand that there is a great difference between Thought-Waves sent forth idly and unconsciously, and without knowledge of the underlying laws of Mental Influence, and those projected with a full knowledge of the laws governing the phenomena and urged on and directed by a powerful Will of the sender. The force is the same, but the degree of its power, and the measure of its effects are determined by the conditions of its sending force.

The vibratory force of these Thought-Waves does not cease with the sending forth of the wave, but persists for a long time afterward. Just as heat in a room persists long after the fire in the stove has been extinguished — just as the perfume of the flower exists in a room long after the flower has been removed — just as a ray of light travels through space for millions of miles, and for centuries after the star itself has been blotted out of existence — just as any and all forms of vibratory energy persist in manifesting after the initial impulse has been withdrawn — so do the vibrations of Thought continue long after the thought, yes, long after the brain which sent them forth has passed into dust.

There are many places today filled with the thought-vibrations of minds long since passed outside of the body. There are many places filled with the strong vibrations of tragedies long since enacted there. Every place has an atmosphere of its own, arising from the thought vibrations set in motion by the various persons who have inhabited or occupied them. Every city has its own mental atmosphere, which has an effect upon persons moving into them. Some are lively, some dull, some progressive, some old-fogeyish, some moral, some immoral — the result of the character of the early settlers and leading spirits of the places. The atmosphere affects persons moving into these towns, and either sinks to the general level, or else, if strong enough, help to change the mental tone of the place. Sometimes a change in conditions brings a large influx of new people to the town, and the mental waves of the newcomers tend to bring about a marked change in the local mental atmosphere. These facts have been noted by many observing people who were, perhaps, not familiar with the laws and principles underlying the phenomena.

Many have of course noticed the differing atmosphere of stores, offices and other places of business. Some of such places give one an air of confidence and trust; others create a feeling of suspicion and mistrust; some convey an impression of active, wide awake management, while others impress one as being behind the times and suffering from lack of alert, active management. Did you ever stop to think that these different atmospheres were caused by the prevailing mental attitudes of those in charge of the places? The managers of business places send forth Thought-Waves of their own, and their employees naturally falling into the pace set for them, sending forth similar vibrations, and before long the whole place is vibrating on a certain scale. Let a change in the management occur and see what a change soon manifests itself.

Did you ever notice the mental atmospheres of the houses you happened to visit? You may experience and recognize all of the varying notes in the mental scale of their occupants. From some thresholds harmony manifests itself, while others breathe in harmony as soon as you step over the threshold. Some radiate mental warmth, while others seem as cold as an iceberg. Think for a moment and recall the various houses or places you visit, and see how the mental vibrations of the inmates manifest themselves to a visitor.

The low quarters of our cities, the dens of vice and haunts of dissipation vibrate with the character of thought and feeling of those inhabiting them. And the weak-willed visitor is thus tempted. And, in the same way, certain places are filled with strong, helpful, elevating vibrations, which tend to lift up and elevate those coming within their circle of influence. Thoughts and Feelings are contagious, by reason of the Law of Vibration and Mental Induction. When this law is understood the individual is enabled to protect and improve himself. Such Knowledge brings Strength.

Mental Induction

As we stated in the preceding chapter, the phenomena of Mental Influence bears a striking analogy to that of the electrical or magnetic energy. Not only is this so in the phase of wave motion and transmission, but also in the phase of induction, as we shall see presently.

In physical science the term Induction is used to indicate that quality in a manifestation of energy which tends to reproduce in a second object the vibrations manifesting in the first object, without direct contact between the two bodies. A magnet will induce magnetism in another object removed from its space. An electrified object will tend to produce similar vibrations in another object by induction, over great spaces. Heat waves travel along the ether, and tend to produce heat vibrations in objects far removed, notably in the case of the sun and the earth. Even sound waves will affect other objects in this way, as in the well-known instance of the glass or vase "singing" in response to the musical note sounded afar off. In fact, we see and hear by processes similar to those described.

And in this same manner that Thought-Waves carry the vibrations of the mind sending them forth to great distances, or lesser ones, tending to set up similar vibrations in the middle of other persons within their field force. Thus a person feeling a strong degree of anger will pour forth waves of that degree of mental vibration, which, coming in contact with the brains of other persons, tend to set up a similar feelings or emotions and thus cause the person to "feel cross" or "peevish" or even to manifest a similar angry state of mind. We all know how easily a fight is started by a very angry person in a room sending forth violent vibrations. One has but to remember the instances of mob violence to see how easily the "contagion of hate and anger" spread among people who allow themselves to be influenced. And not only is this true of undesirable emotions and feelings, but also of desirable ones. The influence of a good man who happens to be strong mentally spreads among those around him, influencing in them for good.

Orators, actors, preachers and teachers send forth strong within toll currents, which tend to produce mental conditions on the part of their hearers corresponding to the feeling held by the mind of the speaker. When you remember how this speaker swayed your feelings, or how that actor made you weep with pity, shiver with fear, or laugh with joy, you will see how Mental induction acts.

But not only is this true when we are in the actual presence of the person sending out the Thought-Waves, but it is equally true that we are influenced by persons far removed from us in space, often without their knowledge or intent, although sometimes (in the case of one who understands the principal most) with full knowledge and intent.

The ether with which space is filled carries these Thought-Waves in all directions, and the surface of the earth, particularly in the densely occupied portions, is filled with these waves. These waves, carrying the mental vibrations, coming in contact with each other, tend to set up combinations on one hand, or else neutralize each other on the other hand. That is to say, if two sets of waves of a similar nature meet there is likely to be a combination formed between them just as between two chemicals having an affinity for each other. In this way the "mental atmosphere" of places, towns, houses, etc., is formed. On the other hand if currents of opposing vibrations came in contact with each other, there will be manifested a conflict between the two, in which each will lose in proportion to its weakness, and the result will be either a neutralization of both or else a combination having vibrations of an average rate. For instance, if two currents of mental energy meet, one being a thought of Love and the other Hate, they will neutralize each other if they are equal, or if one is stronger than the other, it will persist but robbed of much of its strength. If it were not for this neutralizing effect we would be largely at the mercy of stray currents of thought. Nature protects us in this way, and also by rendering us immune to a considerable extent.

But nevertheless we are affected by these waves to a considerable extent, unless we have learned to throw them off by knowledge of the laws and an enforcement of them by practice. We all know how great waves of feeling spread over the town, city or country, sweeping people off their balance. Great waves of political enthusiasm, or War spirits, or prejudice for or against certain people, or groups of people, sweep over places and cause men to act in a manner that they will afterward regret when they come to themselves and consider their acts in cold blood. Demagogues will sway them or magnetic leaders who wish to gain their votes or patronage; and they will be led into acts of mob violence, or similar atrocities, by yielding to these waves of "contagious" thought. On the other hand we all know how great waves of religious feeling sweep over a community upon the occasion of some great "revival" excitement or fervor.

The effect of these Thought-Waves, so far as the power of induction is concerned, of course depends very materially upon the strength of the thought or feeling being manifested in the mind sending them forth. The majority of persons put but little force into the mental manifestations, but here and there is to be found a thinker whose Thought-Waves are practically "a stream of living will" and which of course have a very strong inductive effect upon the minds of others with whom the waves come in contact. But it likewise follows that a number of persons thinking along the same lines will produce a great volume of power by a combination of their thought currents into great streams of mental force.

Then again there is another feature of the case that we must not lose sight of, and that is the Attraction between minds, by virtue of which one draws to himself the Thought-Waves of others whose thoughts are in accord with his own. The contrary is true, for there is Repulsion between the minds of persons and the Thought-Waves of others whose thoughts are not in accord with his own. The contrary is true, for there is Repulsions between the minds of persons and the Thought-Waves of others antagonistic to their thoughts. To quote a well-worn and much-used expression to illustrate this truth, "Like attracts Like," and "Birds of a Feather flock together." There is ever in operation this marvelous law of Attraction and Repulsion of Mental Energy— Persons allowing their thoughts to run along certain lines, and permitting the feelings to be expressed in certain ways, draw to themselves the Thought-Waves and mental influences of others keyed to the same mental key-note. And likewise they repel the waves and influences of an opposing nature. This is an important fact to remember in one's everyday life. Good attracts Good and repels Evil. Evil attracts Evil and repels Good. The predominant Mental Attitude serves to attract similar influences and to repel the opposing ones.

Therefore watch carefully the character and nature of your thoughts — cultivate the desirable ones and repress the undesirable ones. Verily "As a man thinketh in his heart, so is he."

Some Thought-Waves sent forth with but little strength travel slowly and do not proceed very far from their place of emanation, but creep along like some smoke or fog, lazily and yielding. Other thoughts charged with a greater intensity of desire or will, dart forth vigorously like an electric spark, and often travel great distances. The weak Thought-Waves do not last a very long time, but fade away or become neutralized or dissipated by stronger, forces. But the strong thoughts persist for a long time, retaining much of their vitality and energy.

In the same manner the Thought-Waves of a person will continue to vibrate around him wherever he goes, and those coming in contact with him will be impressed by the character of his vibrations in this way. Some men send forth gloomy vibrations in this way. Some men send forth gloomy vibrations, which you feel when you come in contact with them. Others radiate good-cheer, courage and happiness, which conditions are induced in those with whom they come in contact. Many people will manifest these qualities so strongly that one can notice the effect the moment such persons enter a room. They carry their atmosphere with them, and the same is induced in the minds of others around them.

In the same way some people carry with them vibrations of Will-Power and Masterfulness that beat upon the minds of others, making them feel the power of such persons and conquering their own will-power and changing their desires. Others manifest a strong power of Fascination or Attraction, in a similar manner which tends to draw others to them and to their desires and wishes. Not only does this principle operate in the phase of general mental atmospheres, but also in the phase of direct personal influence.

All forms of Mental influence operate along the lines of Mental induction, as herein described. The principle is the same in all cases and instances, although the manner of operation varies according to the particular phase of the phenomena manifested. Remember this as we proceed, and you will be able to understand the subject much better.

MENTAL CONCENTRATION

The two principal factors in the manifestation of Mental Influence, in all of its forms, are what are know as (1) Concentration, and (2) Mental Imagining. The first of these factors shall be considered in this chapter, the succeeding chapter taking up the consideration of the second.

"Concentration" is a word derived from two Latin words, i.e., "con," a prefix meaning " to;" and "centrum," meaning "center" or "fixed central point." The two words combined mean, literally, "to bring to a common point; to focus," etc. Thus the word "Concentration" is seen to mean, literally, "the act or state of bringing to a fixed point or focus.

Borrowing an analogous illustration from physical science, we readily see that the highest forms of energy, force or power are manifested by bringing the force to a focus, center, or common point thereby directing to that point the entire energy employed, instead of allowing it to become dissipated over a larger area. The electricity generated by a battery or dynamo, if allowed to diffuse itself over a large surface manifests but a small degree of the power that may be obtained from it by compelling it to discharge itself from a small point of focus. The same is true regarding the power of steam, which manifests great power by being forced to discharge itself

through a small point or opening instead of being permitted to spread itself widely in the air. The same law applies to gunpowder, which manifests force by its gases being compelled to escape through the small gun-barrel instead of spreading in all directions, which it would do if unconfined. Another familiar example is that of the sun glass, or "burning-glass," which brings the rays of the sun to a common point or focus, greatly intensifying the heat and light by reason thereof.

The occult masters have ever impressed upon their pupils the importance and necessity of acquiring the power of Mental Concentration, and all trained and developed occultists have practiced and persevered toward this end, the result being that some of them attained almost miraculous mental powers and influence. All occult phenomena are caused in this way, and all occult power depends upon it. Therefore the student of Mental Influence should devote much thought, time and practice to this most important branch of the subject.

It is a fact known to all students of mental phenomena that very few persons possess more than a very small degree of concentration. They allow their mental forces to become scattered and dissipated in all directions, and obtain little or no results from the same. In the degree that a man is able to concentrate, so is he able to manifests mental power. A man's power of mental concentration is to a great extent his measure of greatness.

Mental Concentration, in practice, consists of focusing the mind upon a given subject, or object, firmly and fixedly, and then holding it there for a certain time, fully intent upon its object, and not allowing itself to be diverted or attracted from its object. It likewise consists in the correlative power of then detaching the mind from that subject, or object, and either allowing it to rest, or else focusing it upon another object. In other words, it either gives undivided attention or else inhibits (or "shuts off") attention from the given subject or object.

To the reader who has had no experience along the lines of Mental Concentration, it may seem like a very easy Mental Influence task to focus the mind upon a subject, and then hold it there firmly and fixedly. But a little practice will undeceive such a person and will bring him to a realizing sense of the difficulty of the task. The mind is a very restless thing, and its tendency is to dance from one thing to another, darting here and there, soon tiring of continued attention, and like a spoiled child, seeking a new object upon which to exercise itself .On the other hand, many people allow their minds to concentrate (involuntarily) upon whatever may strike their fancy, and, forgetting everything else, they give themselves up to the object attracting their attention for the moment, often neglecting duties and important interests, and becoming day dreamers instead of firm thinkers. This involuntary concentration is a thing to be avoided, for it is the allowing of the attention to escape the control of the will. The Mental Concentration of the occultists is a very different thing, and is solely in control of the will, being applied when desirable, and taken off or inhibited when undesirable.

The trained occultist will concentrate upon a subject or object with a wonderful intensity, seemingly completely absorbed in the subject or object before him, and oblivious to all else in the world. And yet, the task accomplished or the given time expired, he will detach his mind from the object and will be perfectly fresh, watchful and wide-awake to the next matter before him. There is a difference in being controlled by involuntary attention, which is a species of self- hypnotizing, and the control of the attention, which is an evidence of mastery.

The secret of Mental Concentration lies in the control of the Attention. And the control of the Attention lies in the exercise of the Will.

A celebrated French psychologist has well said: "The authority is subject to the superior authority of the Ego. l yield it or I withhold it as I please. l direct it in turn to several points. l concentrate it upon each point as long as my will can stand the effort." Sully says: "Attention may be roughly defined as the active self-direction of the mind to any object which presents itself at the moment."

All of the occult authorities begin teaching their pupils Attention as the first step toward Mental Concentration. They instruct the pupil to examine some familiar object, and endeavor to see as many details as possible in the object. Then after hearing the pupil's report, the master sends him back to the task, bidding him seek for new details, and so on until at last the pupil has discovered about all concerning the object that can be discovered. The next day a new object is given to him, and the process is repeated. First simple objects are given, and then more complex ones, until at last objects of great complexity are easily mastered. In this way not only is the power of close observation highly developed, but also the faculty of Attention becomes so highly strengthened that the pupil is able to exert the greatest amount of Mental Concentration with scarcely the consciousness of effort. And such a person then becomes a very giant in the manifestation of Mental Influence. For he is able to mold his mind "one-pointed," as the Orientals describe it, until he has focused and directed a mighty degree of Mental Influence toward the desired object.

Among the practices imposed upon their pupils by occult masters may be named Mathematics, Drawing, Analysis, etc. You will readily see why this is. To begin with, Mathematics requires the undivided attention of the student — unless he concentrates upon his examples, he will not be able to work out their solution. And, according to the principle in Nature that "practice makes perfect," and that "exercise develops power," the practice of the mind along lines requiring voluntary attention and mental concentration will inevitably result in the acquirement of the mental control and power, which renders possible the strongest manifestation of Mental Influence.

The person who uses Mental Influence must certainly possess the power of focusing the force to a common point, in order to manifest the greatest amount of power and influence. And that faculty of focusing results from the training of the mind along the lines of Concentration. And Concentration arises from the mastery of Voluntary Attention. So there you have the whole matter in a nutshell. So your first step toward acquiring Mental Influence should be to cultivate Voluntary Attention.

We might fill page after page with exercises designed to strengthen your faculty of Voluntary Attention, but what would be the use? The best plan is to set you to work to find something upon which to concentrate, for the very search will develop attention. Look around you for some object to study in detail. Then concentrate your attention upon it until you have seen all there is about it to be seen, then take up another object and pursue the practice further. Take a page — this page, if you will, and count the number of words on it. Then see how many words are required to fill each line, on an average, then see how many letters there are in each word, in each line, on the whole page. Then go over the page and see if any words are misspelled, or if any of the letters are imperfect, etc. In short, get acquainted with this page, until you know all about it. Then take up another page, and after studying it in the same way, compare the two. And so on. Of course this will be very dry and tedious unless you take an interest in it. And, remembering just what the exercise is designed for may arouse this interest. After practicing this way for a short time each day, you will begin to find that you are able to bestow greater attention upon objects upon which you are trying to manifest Mental Influence. You are developing Concentration, and that is the great secret of the use of Mental Influence, and explains the difference in its manifestation among men. Think over this.

MENTAL IMAGING

In our last chapter we called your attention to the first of the two principal factors in the manifestation of Mental Influence, namely, "Mental Concentration." In the present chapter we shall consider the second factor tending to render possible the said manifestation, namely, "Mental Imaging."

What is known as a "Mental Image, in occultism, is the mental creation, in the imagination of a "picture" of the things, events or conditions that one desires to be manifested or, materialized in actual effect. A moments thought will show you that unless you know "just what" you desire, you can take no steps toward attaining it on any plane of manifestation. And the more clearly your desires are perceived in your imagination, the clearer is the work of proceeding toward the realization of that desire. A Mental Image gives you a framework upon which to work. It is like the drawing of the architect, or the map of the explorer. Think over this for a few moments until you get the idea firmly fixed in your mind.

And now the same rule holds well on the plane in which the manifestation of Mental influence takes place. The occultist first builds up, in his imagination, a Mental Image or Picture of the conditions he wishes to bring about, and then by concentrating his influence strongly, instead of in a haphazard way as is the case with the majority of people who do not understand the laws and principles underlying the manifestations of the forces of mind. The Mental Image gives shape and direction to the forces, which is being concentrated upon the desired object or subject. It may be compared to the image on the glass of the Magic Lantern, through which the focused rays of the lamp pass, the result being that a corresponding image is reproduced upon the screen or curtain beyond. The analogy is a very close one indeed, if we remember that the minds of the majority of people are more or less blank screens or curtains upon which play the pictures produced there by outside influences, suggestions, environments, etc., for very few people realize their individuality, and are merely reflections of the thoughts and ideas of other people.

An eminent authority, Sir Francis Galton, who was one of the leading authorities upon psychology of preceding generations, has said on this subject: "The free action of a high visualizing faculty is of much importance in connection with the higher processes of generalized thought. A visual image is the most perfect form of mental representation whatever the shape, position and relations of objects to space are concerned. The best workmen are those who visualize the whole of what they propose to do before they take a tool in their hands. Strategists, artists of all denominations, physicists who contrive new experiments, and in short, all who do not follow routine, have a need for it. A faculty that is of importance in all technical and artistic occupations, that gives accuracy to our perceptions and justice to our generalizations, is starved by lazy disuse instead of being cultivated judiciously in such a way as will, on the whole, bring the best return. l believe that a serious study of the best way of developing and utilizing this faculty, without prejudice to the practice of abstract thought in symbols, is one of the many pressing desires in the yet unformed science of education."

And what Galton has said of the value of the use of this faculty of the mind in the affairs of the material plane, so it is likewise true of the manifestations on the mental plane. You know that the clearer a Mental Picture you possess of anything that you want — the better you know just what you want — and the better you know the latter, the better able you are to take steps to get it. Many people go through life wanting "something," but not really knowing "just what" they do want. ls it any wonder that they do not realize or materialize their desires any better? And the same thing holds well on the plane of manifestation of Mental Influence. If one wishes to materialize anything by the use of the influence, is he not handicapped by a lack of Mental Image of just what he wants to materialize, and is he not helped very much by the creation of a mental "pattern" or plan, in the shape of a mental picture, through and around which he may direct his thought-currents?

The occultists manifesting the greatest degree of Mental Influence acquire by practice this art of creating Mental Images of that which they wish to materialize.They train their Imagination in this way until the very act of creating the Mental Image acts strongly toward the actual materialization or event, as "actually existing" in their minds before they attempt to concentrate their Thought-Waves upon the task of accomplishing it. Then the Mental Picture, being completed and standing in strong outline, they focus their mental force through it, just as in the case of the magic lantern before referred to, and the picture is reproduced on the screen of mentality of other people.

The imagination may be strengthened in many ways, the principle being constant and persistent practice. The practice of recalling to the memory of scenes previously witnessed, and then whether describing them to others or else drawing a rough picture of them will help in this matter. Describe to others scenes that you have witnessed, occurrences. details of appearances, etc. etc., until you are able to reproduce mentally the aspects and appearances of the things. Then you may begin to draw mental pictures of things desired as if they were being drawn on the screen of your mind. See, mentally, the things as actually occurring — create a little playhouse of your own, in your mind, and there enact the plays that you wish to witness in actual life. When you have acquired this, you will be able to project your mental pictures on the screen of objectivity in actual life with far greater effect.

In thinking of this subject, you would do well to remember the illustration of the magic lantern, for the figure is a good one, and will enable you to carry the idea better in your mind. You see, in giving you this suggestion, we are really telling you to form a mental picture of the mental magic lantern, using the illustration given — you see how much easier it is for you to think of it in this way and how much easier it is for you to manifest it in practice.

Build your Mental Images by degrees, commencing with the general outlines, and then filling in the details. Always commence by trying simple and easy things, and then working up to the more complex and difficult feats.

And now, I offer a word of warning at this point to all. Do not allow your imagination to "run away with you" — do not became a dreamer of dreams and a doer of nothing. You must master your imagination and make it your servant and not your master. You must make it do your bidding, instead of allowing it to dictate to you.

You will see in the succeeding chapters the important part that Mental Imaging plays in the different phases of Mental Influence. Even when we do not refer directly to it by name, you will see that the "idea" sought to be conveyed by one mind to another — the feeling, desire or mental state sought to be transferred from one mind to others — must and does depend very materially for strength upon the dearness and completeness of the Mental Image held in the mind of the person seeking to do the influencing, the "projector" of the Mental Image of his mental magic lantern, upon the screen of the minds of others. Carry this principle well in mind that you may see its operation in the different forms.

Fascination

In this and the next chapter we shall present to you information regarding the effect of Mental Influence manifested when there is personal contact between the persons using the power and the person affected. Then we shall pass on to a consideration of the effect produced when the persons are not in direct contact with each other.

There are two general forms of the direct use of Mental Influence, which, although somewhat resembling each other, may still be separated into two classes. The first we shall call "Fascination" and the second "Hypnotism."

By Fascination we mean the manifestation of Mental Influence when the two persons are together, without passes or the usual hypnotic methods. By Hypnotism we mean the use of the power, also, when the two parties are together, but accompanied by passes or hypnotic methods.

Under the head of Fascination are to be found the manifestations generally known as "Personal Magnetism," "Charming," etc., is quite commonly employed, in varying degrees by many persons, often without their conscious knowledge of the principles employed. Many persons are possessed of the power of Fascination "naturally" and without having studied or practiced the principles. Many others, not originally possessing the power, have acquired by study and practice the power to influence people in this way. For, it must be known, the power may be acquired by study and practice just as may any other power of mind and body. To some it is easy, to others difficult — but all may acquire a very great degree of the power by intelligent study and practice of the underlying principles.

Fascination is one of the oldest forms of the manifestations of Mental Influence. It was known to, and employed by, the earliest races of men. It is even found among the lower animals that pursue their prey or capture their mates by its use. A recent writer on the subject has defined the word, used in this connection, as: "Acting upon by some powerful or irresistible influence;

influencing by an irresistible charm; alluring, exciting, irresistibly or powerfully, charming, captivating or attracting powerfully, influencing the imagination, reason or will of another in an uncontrollable manner; enchanting, captivating or alluring, powerfully or irresistibly."

As we have just said, this power is observable even among the lower animals in some cases. Instances are related by naturalists, which scorpions have fascinated other insects, causing them to circle around and around until finally the insect would plunge down right within striking distance of the scorpion, which would then devour its prey. Birds of prey unquestionably fascinate their game, and men who have been brought in contact with wild tigers, lions, etc., have testified that they felt paralyzed in some manner, their legs refusing to obey their will, and their minds seeming to become numbed and stunned. Those who have seen a mouse in the presence of a cat will testify to the effect of some power exerted by the latter. Birds in the presence of a cat and serpents also manifest symptoms of a conquered will. And naturalists cite many instances of the employment of this force by birds seeking to captivate and charm their mates at the beginning of the season.

Among men it has been noticed that certain individuals possess this power to a great degree. Some of the "great men" of ancient and modem times having been so filled with the power that they could manage their followers almost as one would move automatons. Julius Caesar had this power developed to a great degree, and used it from youth to his last days. He was worshipped — almost as a god by his soldiers — who would undertake almost any task at his bidding. Napoleon also possessed this charm to a wonderful degree. It enabled him to control men with whom he came in contact, and to bend them to his will. He rose from a poor student to the dignity and power of the Emperor of France. When banished to Elba he escaped, and landing in France, alone and unarmed, confronted the ranks of the French army drawn up to capture him, and walking towards the soldiers compelled the latter to throw down their guns and flock to his support. He entered Paris at the head of the great army, which had been sent forth to capture him. This is no wild legend, but a sober fact of history. And in our own times we see how certain leaders of men sweep people before them and move them around like pawns on the chessboard of life.

All of the above mentioned phenomena comes under the head of Fascination, and is the result of the emanation of streams of active Thought-Waves from the mind of a person, the same being strongly concentrated and directed toward those whom the person wishes to affect. The person forms a strong thought in his mind and sends it out to the others charged with the force of concentrated will, so that the other person feels it most strongly and forcibly. The fundamental idea is the forming of the thought, and then sending it out to the other person.

For instance, if you wish a person to like you, you should form in your mind this thought: "That person likes me," fixing it in your own mind as a fact. Then project to him the concentrated thought, "You like me — you like me very much," with an air of assurance and confidence, and the other person is bound to feel the effect unless he or she has acquired a knowledge of the subject and is using self-protection. The thought should be sent forth with the strength that usually accompanies a strong spoken statement, but you must not actually "speak" the words aloud — you should merely say them strongly "in your mind."

If you wish to produce an effect or impress Strength upon another person, the same process may be used, changing the Thought and vibrations to the idea that you have a stronger Will than the other person, and are able to overcome his Will — using the silent message of "I am Stronger than you — my Will overcomes yours,"

Some successful agents and salesmen use the following method in reaching their customers. They form a thought that the other person desires their goods very much, and then they send out the Thought-Waves that "You desire my goods — you want them very much — you have an irresistible longing for them," etc.

Others use the following when they wish another to comply with their wishes: "You will do as I say — will do as I say — you will yield to me fully and completely," etc.

You will readily see from the above examples that the whole principle employed in any and all of these cases consists of:

(1) The Thought of what the person wishes the other to do held firmly in the mind; and

(2) The projection of that Thought to the other, silently, in the shape of unspoken words.

In the above you have the whole secret of Fascination condensed to a small space. You will understand of course, that the words are only a means of concentrating and vitalizing the thought. Animals merely feel Desires, but are able to fascinate by the strength of them, although they cannot use words. And one person may fascinate another without understanding a word of his language, the real strength coming from the strength of the desire behind the words. The formation of the desire-thought into words, is merely for the purpose of concentrating and focusing the thought, for words are concentrated symbols of ideas, thoughts or feelings.

The exact process of "sending forth" the Thought-Wave to the other is difficult to describe. You know how you feel when you say something very forcible and emphatic to another person. You can fairly "feel" the force of the words being hurled at the other person. Well, cultivate that same power in sending forth the "unspoken word" in the above manner, and you will soon be able to notice the effect of the thought on the other. It may help you to imagine that you can see the force flying from you to the other. The imagination properly used helps very much in these matters, for it creates a mental path over which the force may travel.

You must not act awkwardly when sending out the Thought-Waves, but converse in an ordinary manner, sending your Thought-Waves between your speeches, when the other person is talking to you, or at any pause in the conversation. It is always well to send first a powerful Thought-Wave before the conversation is opened, preferably while you are approaching the person. And it is likewise well to terminate the interview with a "parting shot" of considerable strength. You will find that these Thought-Waves are of far greater power than spoken words, and then again, you can in this way send out impressions that you could not utter in spoken words for obvious reasons.

And now do you see how you have been affected by persons who have influenced you at times in your past life? Now that you know the secret you will be in a measure immune from further impressions from others. And when you read our concluding chapter, entitled "Self-Protection," you will be able to surround yourself with a protective armor through which the Thought-Waves cannot penetrate, but which will turn aside the shafts directed toward you.

Hypnotic Influence

As we have mentioned in the previous lesson, there is a general resemblance between the manifestation of Mental Influence, known as "Fascination," and that known as Hypnotic Influence. In the manifestation known as Fascination, the influence is exerted solely by Thought- Waves passing from mind to mind without a physical medium or channel other than the ether. In Hypnotic Influence, on the contrary, the influence is heightened by means of passes, stroking or eye influence.

In Hypnotic Influence the mind of the person affected, whom we shall call the "subject," is rendered passive by a flow of mental energy calculated to render it more or less drowsy or sleepy, and therefore less calculated to set up powers of resistance to the Thought-Waves of the person using the influence. But the power employed is the same in all cases, no matter whether they fall under the classification of Fascination or whether that of Hypnotic Influence. The two classes of manifestation, as a matter of fact, really blend into each other, and it is difficult to draw a dividing line in some cases.

Hypnotic Influence is a form of that which was formerly termed Mesmerism, which name was given to it in honor of its discoverer, Frederick Anton Mesmer, who practiced this form of Mental Influence during the latter half of the Eighteenth Century. As a fact, however, the force and its use was known to the ancients centuries before Mesmer's time, the latter person having merely rediscovered it.

Mesmer taught that the power was based upon the presence of a strange universal fluid which pervaded everything, and which had a peculiar effect upon the nerves and brains of people. He and his followers believed that it was necessary to put the subjects into a sound sleep before they could be influenced. But both of these ideas have given way to the new theories on the subject now held by investigators and students of the subject.

It is now known that the "magnetic fluid" believed in by Mesmer and his followers is nothing else than the currents of

Thought-Waves emanating from the mind of the operator. And it is also known that the "deep sleep" condition is not necessary to render the will of the subject subservient to that of the operator. It is also now known that the nerves of the arms and fingers afford a highly sensitive conductor for the mental currents, which may be propelled over them to the mind of the subject, or to his nerves and muscles. This fact is explained by the well-known scientific fact that the material of which the nerves are composed is almost identical with that of the brain — in fact the nervous system may be spoken of as a continuation of the brain itself. It is now also known that the eye has a peculiar property of transmitting the mental currents along the rays of light entering it and from thence to the eyes of the other person. The above fact explains the phenomena of hypnotic influence, as it is now known to science. The question of "Suggestion" also has a bearing on the subject, as we shall see presently.

Modern operators do not produce the "deep sleep" condition usually except in cases when it is desired to produce some form of psychic phenomena apart from the subject of Mental Influence — that is, in which they are merely inducing the deep hypnotic condition in order to get the subject into a psychic condition in which the phenomena mentioned may be manifested or exhibited. We shall not enter into this phase of the subject in this book, for it is outside of the immediate subject. The modem hypnotic investigator merely induces a passive state in the mind, nerves or muscles of the subject sufficient to reduce the powers of resistance, and then he gives his orders or "verbal suggestions" accompanied by a projection of his Thought-Waves into the mind of the subject.

In order to illustrate the subject, we will give you a few experiments, which may be easily performed by anyone manifesting the power of concentration and thought-projection. There is of course a great difference in the degrees of impressionability of different persons to hypnotic influence — that is to say, difference in degrees of resistance. Some persons will interpose a strong resistance, while others will set up a very feeble resistance, which is easily beaten down by the will of the operator. In the following experiments you had better begin by getting some person who is perfectly willing for the experiment, and who will not interpose a resistance but who is willing to become passive. Some person friendly to you and interested in the experiments, we mean.

Begin by having the person stand before you. Then make sweeping passes in front of the person from head to foot. Then make a few passes in front of the face of the subject, then along his arms. Then take hold of his hands and hold them a little while, looking him straight in the eyes. Make all passes downward. Avoid levity or laughter and maintain a serious, earnest expression and frame of mind.

Then standing in front of the subject tell him to take his will off of his legs and stand perfectly passive and relaxed. Then looking him straight in the eyes, say to him: "Now, I am going to draw you forward toward me by my mental power — you will feel yourself falling forward toward me — don't resist but let yourself come toward me — I will catch you, don't be afraid - now come - come - come - now you're coming, that's right," etc. You will find that he will begin to sway toward you and in a moment or two will fall forward in your arms. It is unnecessary to say that you should concentrate your mind steadily upon the idea of his falling forward, using your will firmly to that effect. It will help matters if you hold your hands on each side of his head, but just in front of him, not touching him, however, and then draw away your hands, toward yourself, saying at the same time: "Come now come — you're coming," etc. Standing behind the subject and drawing him backward may reverse this experiment. Be sure and catch him in your arms when he fails to protect him from a fall to the floor.

In the same manner you may fasten his hands together, telling him that he cannot draw them apart. Or you may start him revolving his hands, and then giving him orders that he cannot stop them. Or you may draw him all around the room after you, following your finger that you have pointed at his nose. Or you may make him experience a feeling of heat and pain by touching your finger to his hand and telling him that it is hot. All of the familiar simple experiments may be performed successfully upon a large percentage of persons, in this way, by following the above general directions. We shall not go into detail of the higher experiments of Hypnotism, as that forms a special subject by itself. We give the above experiments merely for the purpose of showing you that the phenomena of Hypnotic Influence does not require any "magnetic fluid" theory, and is all explainable upon the hypothesis of Mental Influence by means of Thought- Waves and Mental Induction.

In the above experiments, be sure you "take off" the influence afterward, by making upward passes, and willing that the influence pass off. Do not neglect this.

In your experiments, if you care to undertake them, you will soon discover the power of your eye upon the other persons. You will be able to almost feel the force passing from your gaze to theirs. And this is true in the case of the passes and stroking of the hands. You will feel the vibratory waves flowing from your hands into their nervous system. It is wonderful what power is aroused in a person after conducting a few experiments along these lines. Those who care to follow the subject further are referred to a forthcoming book of this series, to be issued shortly, and which will be called "The New Hypnotism," in which full instructions will be given in the higher phenomena, in complete detail.

And now a word of warning — Beware of people who are always putting their hands on you, or patting or stroking you, or wishing to hold your hands a long time. Many persons do this from force of habit, and innocently, but others do so with the intention of producing a mild form of hypnotic influence upon you. If you meet such persons, and find them attempting anything of this sort, you can counteract their influence by sending them a strong thought current (as stated in our last chapter), sending them the thought: "You can't affect me — I am too strong for you — you can't play your tricks on me." It is a good plan to practice this counteracting force when you are shaking hands with a "magnetic" person who seems to affect people. You will soon be able to distinguish these people by a certain force about them and a peculiar expression in their eyes, at the same time using your protective will upon them.

Caution young girls against allowing young men to be too free in using their hands in caressing them, and a word of advice to young men in your family would not be out of place in this respect. There are many cases of sex-attraction, leading to very deplorable results, arising from a conscious or unconscious use of this simple form of Hypnotic Influence. The danger lies in the fact that it renders one passive to other influences, and more readily led into temptation and to yield to the desires or will of the other person. A word to the wise should be sufficient. The use of this power for immoral purposes is a terrible crime and brings down upon the user deplorable results, which all occultists know and teach. Everyone should learn to resist such influences when exerted upon them. Forewarned is Forearmed.

INFLUENCING AT A DISTANCE

In the two preceding chapters we invited your consideration of the manifestation of Mental Influence when the user or projector of the force was in actual contact with, or in presence of, the person or persons he was aiming to influence. In this chapter, and the one immediately following it, we shall pass on to a consideration of the manifestation of the influence when the persons affected are removed in space from the person using the influence.

The general public is familiar in a general way with the phenomena of hypnotism. and to a lesser degree with the phenomena of Fascination in its more common forms of personal Magnetism, etc. But as regards the use of the influence at a distance people are more or less skeptical owing to a lack of knowledge of the subject. And still every day is bringing to the mind of the public new facts and instances of such an influence. and the teaching of various cults along these lines is now awakening a new interest in the subject, and a desire to learn something regarding the laws and principles underlying the same.

As strange as it may appear at first glance, the principles underlying Mental Influence at a distance are precisely the same as those underlying the use of influence when the persons are in the presence of each other. A little thought must show the truth of this. In the case of present influence the mental-currents flow across an intervening space between the two minds — there is a space outside of the two minds to be traversed by the currents. And a moment's thought will show you that the difference between present influence and distant influence is merely a matter of degree — a question of a little more or less space to be traversed by the currents. Do you see this plainly?

Well, then, this being so, it follows that the methods used must be identical. Of course, in the case of personal influence the added effect of the voice, manner, suggestive methods, the eye, etc., are present, which render the result more easily obtained, and causes the "rapport" condition to be more easily established. But with this exception the methods are identical, and even the advantages accruing from the exception mentioned may be duplicated by practice and development in the case of distant influence.

There are a number of methods given by the authorities in this matter of distant influencing, but they are all based upon the same principles named in the previous chapters of this book, i.e. Vibrations, Thought-Waves, Mental Induction, Concentration and Mental Imaging — in these words you have the key to the subject — the rest is all a matter of practice and development, and variation.

One of the most elementary, and yet one of the most effective methods known to occultists is that of creating a Mental Image of the person "treated" (for that is the common term among modern writers on the subject) in the sense of imagining him to be seated in a chair in front of the person treating him at a distance. The treater proceeds to give both verbal commands, and at the same time directs Thought-Waves toward the imaginary person seated before him. This process establishes a psychic condition between the treator and the actual person, although the latter may be removed from the treator by many miles of space. This was the method of the ancient magicians and wonder-workers, and has always been a favorite among persons pursuing these experiments, of desirous, of mentally influencing others at a distance.

A variation of the above, very common in former days, was to mold a clay or wax figure, calling it by the name of the person treated, and identifying it in the mind and imagination with the other person. A variation is also noticed in the cases where a photograph, lock of hair, article of clothing, etc., is used in this way as a psychic connecting link between the two persons. The practitioners of Black Magic, Witchcraft and of her nefarious perversions of Mental influence seemed to prefer these methods, although, on the contrary, they are used with the very best results today by many in giving beneficial treatments to absent patients, friends and others whose welfare is desired. The only effect the Mental Image of the person, or the picture, etc., has is the fact that by these means a psychic connection link is set up along which the Thought- Waves travel more readily.

In the above forms of treatment the treator treats the Mental Image, picture, etc., precisely as he would if the person were actually present. He forgets for the time being that the person may be hundreds of miles away, and concentrates his influence on the image, or picture, etc., because the latter is really the starting point of the psychic chain, which leads direct to the person. The treator sends his Thought-Waves toward the object, and in some cases actually talks (mentally) to the person by means of the medium mentioned. He may give commands, arguments, remonstrance, persuasion, etc., just as if the person were actually present. In short, he acts as if the person were sitting before him, wide-awake, and receptive to his influence.

Another way, employed by some, is to begin darting Thought-Waves toward the other person, forming in the imagination a gradual lengthening "psychic-wire" composed of thought- vibrations. Those practicing this form state that when the psychic-wire is projected sufficiently far (and it travels with incredible speed) and comes in contact with the mind of the other person, the treator feels at once that contact has been established by a peculiar faint "shock" similar to that of a very mild galvanic current. Then the treator proceeds to send his thought-currents along the psychic-wire in the same manner as if the person were actually in his presence, as described under the head of "Fascination, in a preceding chapter. In fact, such treatments, and the others mentioned in this chapter, are really and practically "long distance Fascination."

Another form of distant treatment consists in forming an "astral-tube," mentioned in other books in this series. The astral-tube is set up in a similar manner to the "psychic-wire," and projected toward the person desired to influence. It is formed in the imagination as a "vortex-ring," similar to the little ring of smoke puffed out by the cigar smoker, only larger — about six inches to one foot wide — or, better still, like the ring of smoke ejected from the stack of a locomotive sometimes when it is puffing rapidly. This vortex-ring is then seen, in the imagination, by the use of the will, to lengthen out in the shape of a tube which rapidly extends and travels toward the person treated, in a manner identical with that of the psychic-wire. This tube is known to occultists as the "astral-tube," and is employed in various forms of occult and psychic phenomena, such as clairvoyance and other forms of "Psychomancy," as described by us in our volume of this series, so entitled. Those following this method of distant influencing report that they recognize the completion of the tube by a sensation of stoppage and a feeling of "rapport" having been established between themselves and the other person. In some cases they report that they are able to faintly "see" the figure of the other person in miniature at the other end of the tube, but this is undoubtedly due to the possession of "psycho-mantic" powers, suddenly awakened in to effect. The tube once established the treatment is proceeded with as if they were in the actual presence of the person treated. In many respects the "psychic-wire" and the "astral-tube" methods are similar, and a statement concerning one is generally true of the other.

There are two other methods frequently used in distant influencing which we shall now briefly describe.

The first of these two methods consists in sitting or standing in a quiet place, or rather in some place in which you can concentrate (the advanced occultist can find peace in the midst of the noise) and then directing your Thought-Waves toward the other person, forming in the imagination a mental picture of the force flying from you toward the other, like tiny sparks of electricity, or of a subtle fluid. This mental picture tends to give a concentrative force to the current, which renders them powerful, and sends them direct to the desired spot.

The second of these two methods is that used by the most advanced occultists who have advanced beyond the use of the methods described just now. These people simply stand or sit quietly and concentrate their minds until they attain the state of Mental Calm known to many as "the Silence." Then they create a strong mental picture of the person treated, surrounded by the conditions desired created, or doing the things desired to be done. This is one of the highest forms of Mental Influence and really approaches a higher phase of influence than that of the mental plane as generally known. A picture of a person held in the mind in this way — the person being seen in perfect, robust health, and happy and successful — tends to materialize the same conditions in the person in real life. This form of treatment, however, is possible only to those of great concentration, and who have mastered the act of Mental Imaging, and who also possess Creative Will-Power to a marked degree. Some degree of success in it, however, is open to nearly every student who practices along these lines.

Before practicing any of these experiments, read what we have said in the chapter on "Magic Black and White, and guard against employing the power for evil purposes, for the fate of the Black Magician is a sad one.

INFLUENCING "EN MASSE"

In our last chapter we considered the manifestation of Mental Influence at a distance in so far as was concerned the influencing of one or more persons by another. There is another phase of the subject that must not be overlooked, and that is the influencing of large numbers of people by some active, strong projector of Mental Influence. This form of the manifestation of the power is known as "Mental Influencing En Masse" — "En Masse, of course, means "in a body" — or "in a crowd," and Mental Influencing En Masse means the use of the influence in the phase of exerting a strong attracting or directing power to the mind of "the crowd," or rather, "the public, or a large number of people.

This form of the use of the power is that consciously or unconsciously exerted by the great leaders of men in the fields of statesmanship, politics, business, finance or military life. You will at once recall a number of the so called "great men" of history from ancient times down to our own times who seemed to exert a wonderfully, almost miraculous, effect upon the minds of the people, causing men to see things through the eyes of the strong man, and making of all instruments to carry out the ideals, will or desires of these great masters of Mental Influence. And on a smaller scale are the majority of the successful people who depend upon public support. In fact, this influence in some degree is used by nearly all who succeed in any form of business or profession, in which success calls for the attraction of other people toward the occupation of the person in question. This may seem like a strange thought to many, but occultists know it as the truth, notwithstanding.

The most common form of Influencing En Masse is the lesser degree manifestation, along unconscious lines, manifested by a majority of people by reason of their desire for the success of certain things. By desire we do not mean the mere "wanting" or "wishing" state of mind, but rather that eager longing, craving, demanding mental state that evinces a hungry reaching out for the desired thing. You will notice that the men and women who "get things" are generally those who are possessed of a strong, burning desire for the things in question, which prompts them to be more of less aggressive in the search for satisfaction of the desire possessing them. These people are constantly sending out strong waves of thought-vibrations, which has a drawing, attracting influence upon all with whom they come in contact, and tending to draw such persons toward the center of attraction, which is, of course, the mind of the person sending out such thoughts. And in the same way a person possessed of a strong Fear of a thing will send out similar attracting waves, which have a tendency to attract or draw to him the people calculated to bring about the materialization of the thing feared. This may sound paradoxical, but the secret lies in the fact that in both the case of Desire and Fear the mind forms the Mental Image, which tends to become materialized. Fear, after all, is a form of "expectation," which, alas, too, often tends to materialize it." The thing that I have feared, hath come upon me," says Job, and in that saying he has stated the experience of the race. The way to fight things you may fear is to create a burning desire for the opposite thing.

Other persons who have either studied the principles of Mental Influence, or else have stumbled upon certain facts concerning the same, improve upon this elementary form of Influencing En Masse just mentioned. They send out the Thought-Waves consciously and deliberately, erecting the mental image, and holding strongly to it, so that in time their sweeps of mental currents reach further and further away and bring a greater number of people under the influence and into the field of attraction. They "treat" the public "en masse" by holding the strong mental picture of that which they desire, and then sending out strong thought-currents of desire in all directions, willing that those coming within their radius shall be attracted toward the ideas expressed in the Mental image projected in all directions.

The constant dwelling upon some special object or subject, by men who have developed concentration, strong wills and fixity of purpose, has the effect of sending out from the mind of that person great circles, constantly widening, of Thought-Waves, which sweep ever outward like waves in a pond caused by dropping in a stone. These waves reach and affect a great number of people, and will render them at least "interested" in the object or subject thought of, and the indifference has been overcome. Other appeals to the minds of these people will be far more likely to reach them than otherwise, for "interest" is the first step toward attention, and attention is another step toward action.

Of course, there are very many people sending out circles of Thought-Waves, and these currents come in contact with each other and tend to neutralize each. But now and then a particularly strong man will send out waves that will persist even after meeting other currents, and will reach the minds of the public in spite of the opposition. These thought-currents have the personality of the sender, and reflect the character of his will, be it strong or weak. The Mental Influence sent out by a strong business man in a town will soon make itself felt in a subtle manner, and the store becomes a center of attractive influence, although the public does no understand just why. In the same way some lawyers spring into public favor, although not possessing greater ability than their legal brethren. And popular preachers make their influence felt in a community in similar ways, although often they are not conscious of just what force they are using, their only knowledge being that they have a feeling of inward strength and an attractive influence over people, and at the same time a burning ardent desire to draw people their way, and a strong will to back it up with. And these are just the mental qualities that create and manifest the strongest kind of Mental Influence. And besides, these people almost invariably "know just what they want" — there is no mere vague "wishing" about them — they make a clear mental picture of the things that they wish to bring about, and then they bend every effort toward materializing the picture. Everything they do towards accomplishing their ends gives an additional impetus to their constantly widening and constantly strengthening circle of power and influence.

Some masters of this art of influencing the public create a mental picture of themselves sending out great volumes of Thought-Waves for a time, and then afterward mentally imparting a rotary motion to the waves, until at last they form a mental whirlpool rushing round and round and always sucking in toward the center. An effort of this kind acts on the mental plane just as a physical whirlpool acts on the physical plane, that is it draws into its power all that comes in contact with its force. This is one of the most powerful forms of Influencing En Masse, and is used with great effect by many of the "strong men" of this age; who have acquainted themselves fully with the secrets of the ancient occultists. Ancient Occultism and Modern Finance seem far apart, but they are really working together to further the interests of some of these powerful minds of the day — and the public is paying the bill.

You will readily see from what has been said that an individual who has cultivated the faculty of concentration and has acquired the art of creating sharp, clear, strong mental images, and who when engaged in an undertaking will so charge his mind with the idea of success, will be bound to become an attracting center. And if such an individual will keep his mental picture ever in his mind, even though it may be in the background of his mind, when he is attending to the details and planning of his affairs — if he will give his mental picture a prominent place in his mental gallery, taking a frequent glance at it, and using his will upon it to create new scenes of actual success, he will create for himself a center of radiating thought that will surely be felt by those coming within its field of influence.

Such a man frequently "sees" people coming to him and his enterprises and falling in line with his plans. He mentally "sees" money flowing in to him, and all of his plans working out right. In short, he mentally imagines each step of his plans a little ahead of the time for their execution and he concentrates forcibly and earnestly upon them. It is astonishing to witness how events, people, circumstances and things seem to move in place in actual life as if urged by some mighty power to serve to materialize the conditions so imaged in the mind of the man. But, understood, there has got to be active mental effort behind the imaging. Daydreamers do not materialize thought — they merely dissipate energy. The man who converts thought in activity and material being, throws energy into the task and puts forth his willpower through the picture on the slide. Without the rays of the will there will be no picture projected, no matter how beautifully the imagination has pictured it. Thoughts pictured in mental images and then vitalized by the force of the desire and will tend to objectify themselves into material beings, That is the whole thing in a nutshell.

THE NEED OF THE KNOWLEDGE

Although the true scientific principles underlying the subject of Mental Influence have been but recently recognized and taught to the general public, still the knowledge is far from being new. The occultists of the old civilizations undoubtedly understood the underlying principles and used them in practice, thus gaining an ascendancy over the masses. And more than this, the masses themselves had a more or less comprehensive knowledge of the working principles of the subject, for we find among all peoples, in all times, records of the use of this power. Under one name or another — under one form or another — Mental Influence has been operated and used from the earliest times. And today, even in the most remote portions of the globe, and among the most savage and barbarous races we find instances of the employment of this force.

The forms of the manifestation of Mental Influence are many and varied. In some cases it manifests under the form of a fascinating, attracting power exerted by some people, which causes such persons to draw or attract other persons to them. Persons are allured or "charmed" by others possessing this power, and their affections are taken captive by this mysterious force. Some persons are spoken of as "fascinating," "possessing powers of charming," having "winning ways," having "great personal magnetism," etc. Others exert another form of the power in the driving of and compelling others to do their bidding, and people speak of them as having "a
compelling will," being able "to work their will" on those around them, possessing "dominating powers," etc. We are also brought face to face with the wonderful effects of "Mental Science" under one form or another, under this name or that term, with the many forms of "treatments" followed by the different schools and cults. Then we read in the pages of history about the mysterious powers recorded under the name of Witchcraft, Hexes, Voodoo's, and Black Magic, including the Hawaiian "Kahuna" work. And turning back the pages of history to Ancient time, Greece, Persia and Egypt, not

to speak of India, ancient and modern, we find innumerable instances of the employment of, and knowledge of, Mental influence in some of its forms.

And although many will seek to deny the fact, scientific investigators and students realize that there is but one real underlying principle under and back of all of the various forms of manifestation. The good results, and the evil results, all arise from the employment of the same force, strange as it may appear at first thought. The secret lies in the fact that this Mental Influence is a great natural force, just as is electricity or any other natural forces, and it may be, and is, used for both good and evil purposes. The electricity which runs out machines, lights our houses and performs countless other beneficent tasks in the service of man is also used to electrocute criminals, and the unfortunate person who touches a "live wire" may be struck with instant death. The sun, which warms our earth and renders life possible, also kills countless persons exposed to its rays on the desert, or even in our large cities. Fire, that great friend of man, which has been one of the most potent factors in the evolution of the race from barbarism to civilization, is also a mighty enemy, destroying both property and lives. Water, that most necessary element, which renders life possible, and which is necessary to grow our grain and to perform countless other good services for us, also acts as an enemy at times, drowning people and sweeping away their homes. Gravitation, which holds all things in place, from suns and stars down to the tiniest atom of matter, also causes people to fall to their death from high places, or brings down on their heads objects from above them. In short, every natural force or power is capable of producing either beneficent or baleful effects to man, according to the circumstances of the case. We recognize these things, and accept them as a law of nature. And yet some would deny the identity of the power of Mental influence as manifested in its good and bad uses.

There will be people who ascribe to God all the good qualities of Mental Influence, and ascribe to the Devil all of its evil uses. These people have primitive minds. Their counterparts are seen in those who would credit God with the helpful rain or sun, and who ascribe to the Devil the same things when there occurs a flood or a drought. Such reasoning is worthy only of the savage mind. The forces are natural forces, and work according to their own laws, imminent in their constituent qualities and nature, and are in that

sense "above good and evil." When they work for man's interest
and comfort man calls them "good" — when they work harm and
discomfort to him man call them "bad" — but the force remains
unchanged, being neither "good" nor "bad." And thus it is with the
power of Mental Influence — it is above "good" and "bad" — it is
a great natural force, capable of being used for either wear or woe
to mankind. But, remember this, there is a difference. While the
force in itself is neither good nor bad the individual who employs
it may be, and it is, "good" or "bad," according to its use. Just as a
man commits a good or bad act when he uses his gun to slay a wild
beast attacking another man, or else turns it upon his brother or
neighbor, as the case may be — so is a man good or bad according
to his use of Mental Influence. The merit or demerit lies in the
intention and purpose of the user, not in the force or power
employed by him. Therein lies the difference.

On all sides of us we may see the manifestation of the possession
of Mental Influence. We see men who are able to sway those
around them in some mysterious and wonderful way, either by
their powers of persuasion of by their dominant will power. Some
spring into prominence and power suddenly, in a way
unaccountable to those who are ignorant of the secret of Mental
Influence. As we have said in a previous chapter, certain people
seem to have "something about them" that makes them attractive
or successful in their relations with other people. The "personal
magnetism" of leaders manifests itself strongly, some having this
power to such an extent that the masses follow them like a great
flock of sheep after the "bell-whether" with the tinkling bell around
his neck.

We have all come in contact with the "agent" or salesman who
managed in some way to sell us things that we did not want and
had no use for, and after he had gone we wondered and wondered
how it all happened. If we had but understood the laws of Mental
Influence this could not have happened. We have all felt ourselves,
at some time or another in our lives, in the presence of individuals
who almost compelled us to do what we knew in our hearts we
should not do. Knowledge of the laws of Mental influence would
have enabled us to overcome the temptation.

And not only in the case of personal interviews have we been
affected. There is a far more subtle and dangerous use of the
power, i.e., in the shape of "distant influence," or "absent
treatment," as it had been called. And the increase in the interest

and knowledge of Occult matters during the past twenty years has resulted in a widely diffused knowledge of this great force, and its consequent employment, worthily and unworthily, by many people who are thereby enabled to gain an influence over their neighbors and fellow men, who are not familiar with the laws of the force. It would surprise many people if they knew that some of the multi-millionaires of the country, and some of its greatest politicians and leaders, were secret students of Occultism, and who were using their forces upon the masses of the people.

Not only this, but there are Schools of Occultism which teach their pupils the theory, practice and art of Mental Influence, under one name or another — under this guise or that — the result being that there are a greater number of people equipped for the use of this force and instructed in the practice of employing it turned out every year than is generally imagined. There are Schools for Salesmanship giving disguised instruction in the art of Mental Influence. Nearly every large concern employing selling agents has private instructors for their men, who teach them the principles of Mental Influence disguised under the name of "Psychology of Business," or some such name.

And besides these, there are a number of people who have studied at the feet of some of the great metaphysical, semi-religious cults of the day, who have received instruction in Mental influence disguised under the name of some creed or religious teachings, who have departed from the moral principles inculcated by their by their teachers, and who are using their knowledge in the shape of "treatments" of other persons for the purpose of influencing them to accede to their wishes or to act so as to bring financial gain to the person giving the treatment. The air is full of this Black Magic today, and it is surely time that the general masses were instructed on this subject. And this is the purpose of this little book, published and sold at a popular price in order to bring it within the reach of the purses of the "plain people," who have been exploited and influenced by those who have acquired a knowledge of the principles of Mental Influence, and who are using it unworthily upon their fellow men.

There is self protection possible to all, and this little book purposes to teach you how to use it.

MAGIC BLACK AND WHITE

The use of the word "Magic" in connection with Mental Influence is quite ancient. Occultists make a clear distinction between the use of Mental Influence in a manner conducive to the welfare of others, and its use in a selfish, base manner calculated to work harm on others. Both forms are common and are frequently mentioned in all occult writings.

White Magic has many forms, both in its ancient manifestations and in these latter days of revived occult knowledge. The use of Mental Influence in this way generally takes the form of kindly "treatments" of persons by others having their welfare at heart. In this particular class fall the various treatments of the several cults and schools of what is known as Mental Science, or similar names. These people make a practice of giving treatments, both "present" and "absent," for the purpose of healing physical ailments and bringing about a normal Physical condition of health and strength. Similar treatments are given by some to bring about a condition of Success to others, by imparting to the minds of such persons the vibrations of courage, confidence, energy, etc., which surely make for success along the lines of material occupation, etc.

in the same way one may "treat" adverse conditions surrounding others, bringing the force of the mind and will to bear on these conditions with the idea of changing the prevailing vibrations and bringing harmony from in-harmony, and success from failure.

The majority of persons, not informed along these lines, are surrounded by a mental atmosphere arising from the prevailing mental states, thoughts, feelings, etc., and also arising from the thought-currents which they have attracted to them by the Law of Mental Attraction. These Mental Atmospheres, when once firmly settled around a person, render it most difficult for him to "break away" from their vibrations. He struggles and fights, but the prevailing vibrations are beating down upon him all the time and must produce a strong effect upon even persons of strong will, unless indeed they have fully acquainted themselves with the laws of Mental influence and have acquired the power of Concentration.

The habit of a lifetime, perhaps, has to be overcome, and besides the constant suggestive vibrations from the mental atmosphere are constantly bringing a pressure to bear upon the person, so that indeed he has a mighty task before him to throw off the old conditions, unaided and alone. And, so, while individual effort is preferable, there comes a time in the lives of many people when "a helping hand," or rather a "helping mind," is of great service and aid.

The person coming to the mental aid of a person needing his or her services is performing a most worthy and proper act. We hear a great deal about "interfering with other people's minds" in such kind and worthy "treatments," but in many cases there is but little real interference done. The work of the helper is really in the nature of neutralizing and dissipating the unfavorable. Mental Influence surrounds the other person, and thereby giving the other person a chance to work out his own mental salvation. It is true that everyone must do his or her own work, but help of the kind above indicated is surely most worthy and proper.

In these White Magic treatments the person giving the treatments forms the Mental Picture of the desired condition in his mind, and then sends his thought-currents to the other person endeavoring to reproduce the Mental Picture in the mind or thought-atmosphere of the other person. The best way of doing this, of course, is to assert mentally that the desired condition actually exists. One may be of great help and aid to others in this way, and there is no good reason why it should not be done.

And now for the reverse side of the shield — We wish it were possible to avoid even a mention of this hateful form and manifestation of Mental Influence, but we feel that ignorance is no protection, and that it is useless and foolish to pursue the policy of the ostrich which sticks its head in the sand when pursued, that not seeing the hunter the latter may not see him. We believe that it is better to look things in the face, particularly where it is a case of "forewarned being forearmed."

It is a fact known to all students of occultism that Black Magic has been frequently employed in all times to further the selfish, base aims of some people. And it is also known to advanced thinkers today that even in this enlightened age there are many who do not scruple to stoop to the use of this hateful practice in order to serve their own ends, notwithstanding the punishment that occultists know awaits such persons.

The annals of history are full of records of various forms of witchcraft, conjuration and similar forms of Black Magic. All the much talked of forms of "putting spells" upon people are really forms of Black Magic, heightened by the fear and superstition of those affected.

One has but to read the history of witchcraft to see that there was undoubtedly some force at work behind all of the appalling superstition and ignorance shown by the people of those times. What they attributed to the influence of people "in league with the devil" really arose from the use of Black Magic, or an unworthy use of Mental Influence, the two things being one. An examination of the methods used by these "witches," as shown by their confessions, gives us a key to the mystery. These "witches" would fix their minds upon other people, or their animals, and by holding a concentrated mental picture there, would send forth Thought-Waves affecting the welfare of the persons being "adversely treated," which would influence and disturb them, and often bring on sicknesses. Of course, the effect of these "treatments" were greatly heightened by the extreme ignorant fear and superstition held by the masses of people at the time, for Fear is ever a weakening factor in Mental influence, and the superstitions and credulity of the people caused their minds to vibrate in such a manner as to render them extremely passive to the adverse influences being directed against them.

It is well known that the Voodoos of Africa, and similar cults among other savage races, practice Black Magic among their people with great effect. Among the natives of Hawaii there are certain men known as "Kahunas," who pray people sick, or well, whichever way they are paid for. These instances could be multiplied had we the space and inclination to proceed further with the matter.

And in our own civilized lands there are many people who have learned the principles of Mental Influence, and who are using the same for unworthy purposes, seeking to injure others and defeat their undertakings, or else trying to bring them around to their own (the "treator's") point of view and inclinations. The modern revival of occult knowledge has operated along two lines. On the one hand we see and hear of the mighty power for good Mental Influence is exerting among the people today, raising up the sick, strengthening the weak, putting courage into the despondent and making successes of failures. But on the other hand the hateful selfishness and greed of unprincipled persons in taking advantage of this mighty force of nature and prostituting it to their own hateful ends, without heeding the dictates of conscience or the teaching of religion or morality. These people are sowing a baleful wind that will result in their reaping a frightful whirlwind on the mental plane. They are bringing down upon themselves pain and misery in the future.

At this point we wish to utter a solemn warning to those who have been, or are tempted, to employ this mighty force for unworthy purposes .The laws of the mental plane are such that "as one sows so shall he reap." The mighty Law of Attraction acts with the accuracy of a machine, and those who seek to entangle others in a net of Mental influence sooner or later are caught by their own snare. The Black Magician involves him to pieces. He is sucked down into the whirlpool of his own making, and is dragged down to the lowest depths. These are not idle remarks, but a statement of certain laws of nature, in operation on the mental plane, which all should know and heed.

And to those who may feel appalled at this mention of the existence and possibilities of Black Magic we would say that there is one thing to be remembered, and that is that GOOD always overcomes EVIL on the mental plane. A good thought always has the power to neutralize the Evil one, and a person whose mind is filled with Love and Faith may combat a multitude whose minds are filled with Hate and Evil. The tendency of all nature is upward and toward Good. And he who would pull it back toward Evil sets himself against the law of Spiritual Evolution, and sooner or later falls a victim to his folly.

And then, remember this: Thought-Waves find entrance only to those minds that are accustomed to think similar thoughts. He who thinks Hate may be affected by Hate thoughts, while he whose mind is filled with Faith and Love is surrounded by a resistant armor which repels the invading waves, and causes them to be deflected, or else driven back to their senders. Bad thoughts, like chickens, come home to roost. Thoughts ace like Boomerangs, in their tendency to return to their sender. To the poison of Black Magic Nature gives the antidote of Right-Thinking.

Self-Protection

The reader of the preceding chapters will see the power of Mental Influence in its various phases of manifestation, and will recognize the possibility of the force being used to influence himself. The question that will naturally arise in the mind of every student and investigator of this important subject, and which comes to all at sometime, is: "How may I protect myself from the use of this power against myself — how may I render myself immune from these influences which may be directed against me?"

It is true that we, and other writers on the subject, have shown you that one is far less liable to influence if he will maintain a mental atmosphere of high vibration — that is keeping oneself surrounded by a thought atmosphere filled with vibrations of the highest kind of thoughts and free from thoughts and desire of a base, selfish character, which tends to attract similar thoughts. In this way one creates a state of mental hygienic cleanliness which renders him immune from the "contagious thoughts of the selfish plane of desire," etc. This should be remembered and taken advantage of by everyone, for just as physical cleanliness gives no congenial lodgment for the germs of disease, so mental cleanliness refuses to admit the mental microbes.

But there is a method far more efficacious than even the above-mentioned plan. And this method is really that employed by the adepts in Occultism, and the method and practice taught the initiates of the occult brotherhoods and lodges all over the world. Let us consider it here.

In the first place, without entering into a statement of the details of the high occult teachings, we wish to inform you that the Basic Principle of all such teaching and instruction is the fact that within each of us, in the very center of the being of each individual — in the very heart of hearts of the immortal Ego — is what occultists know as the Flame of the Spirit. This is what you recognize in consciousness as the "I *am*" consciousness — that consciousness of being which is far above the consciousness of Personality, or the things of personality. It is that consciousness which informs each individual, unmistakably, that he IS actually an Individual Being. This consciousness comes to the individual by reason of his contact with the great One Life of the Universe — it is the point of contact between the *part* and the *all*.

And in this part of a man's consciousness, coupled with the sense of *being* and "I," there resides a spark from the Divine Flame of Life and Power, which is what has been called the *will* of man. Now, do not mistake us and confuse this with the so called Will of personality, which is merely a Desire, or else a certain firmness, which often is little more than Stubbornness. This inner Will is Real Power, and when once recognized may be drawn upon as a source of unending and unfailing Strength. The occult adepts have developed the consciousness of this Power Within, and use it freely. This is the result of years of practice, and correct living and thinking. But, still, each and every person may draw upon this source of strength within them to aid them in life and to repel the thought-vibrations of the lower plane.

This consciousness may be developed by a realization of its existence, and by a practice of bringing the idea in everyday consciousness, by thought, meditation and practice. The very fact of having called your attention to its existence has awakened within the mind of You who are reading these lines a new strength and sense of power. Think a moment and see whether you do not feel a dawning sense of Strength within you that you have not realized so fully before this moment! A continued recognition in your everyday consciousness of this Something Within will develop your ability to manifest it. Particularly in an hour of need will it spring to your assistance, giving you a sense of a part of yourself crying out to you in words of encouragement: "I Am Here! Be Not Afraid!"

It is very difficult to give you this method in written or printed works, but if you will enter fully into a recognition of this Inward Power you will find yourself developing a new power of resisting outside influences that will astonish you.

When you come in contact with people who are seeking to influence you in any of the ways mentioned in the preceding chapters of this book, or in others ways, you will find yourself able to defy their mental attacks by simply remembering the strength imminent in your "I," aided by the statement (made silently to yourself): "l am an Immortal Spirit, using the Will within my Ego." With this Mental Attitude you may make the slightest mental effort in the direction of throwing out from your mind vibrations, which will scatter the adverse influences in all directions, and which, if persisted in, will cause the other person to become confused and anxious to let you alone.

With this consciousness held in mind, your mental command to another, "Let me alone — I cast off your influence by the power of my Spirit," will act so strongly that you will be able to actually see the effect at once. If the other person is stubborn and determined to influence you by words of suggestion, coaxing, threatening, or similar methods, look him or her straight in the eyes, saying mentally "I defy you — my inner power casts off your influence. Try this the next time that anyone attempts to influence you either verbally or by Thought-Waves and see how strong and positive you will feel, and how the efforts of the other person will fail. This sounds simple, but the little secret is worth thousands of dollars to every individual who will put it into practice.

Above all, put out of your mind all Fear of others persons. The feeling of fear prevents you from manifesting the power within you to its full extent. Cast out fear as unworthy and hurtful.

Not only the case of personal influence in the actual presence of the other person may be defeated in this way, but the same method will act equally as well in the matter of repelling the mental influence of others directed against you in the form of "absent treatments," etc. If you feel yourself inclining toward doing something which in your heart you feel that is not to your best interests, judged from a true standpoint, you may know that, consciously or unconsciously someone is seeking to influence you in this way. Then smile to yourself and make the statements mentioned above, or some similar one, and holding the power of the Spirit within your "I" firmly in you mind, send out a mental command just as you would in the case of the actual presence of the person himself or herself. You may also deny the influencing power out of existence by asserting mentally: "I *deny* your power to influence me — you have no such power over me — I am resting on my knowledge of Spirit and its Will within me — I deny your power out of existence." This form of denial may be used either in the case of absent influence or personal influence. The rule is the same in all cases.

In repelling these absent influences you will at once experience a feeling of relief and strength and will be able to smile at the defeated efforts of the other person. If you feel sufficiently broad and full of love for mankind you may then "treat" the other person for his error, sending him thoughts of Love and Knowledge with the idea of dispelling his ignorance and selfishness, and bringing him to a realization of the higher truths of life.

You will doubtless have many interesting experiences arising from thus repelling these attacks. In some cases you will find that the next time you meet the person in question he will appear confused and puzzled and ill at ease. In other cases the person will begin to manifest a new respect and regard for you, and disposed to aid you instead of trying to influence you to his way and desire. In other cases the person will still have the desire, and will endeavor to "argue" you into doing that which he has tried to influence you into doing by Mental Influence, but his efforts will "fall flat," and without effect, particularly if you give him "another dose of the assertion of the Power of the Spirit within you.

In the same way you should call upon your Higher Self for aid and strength when you feel yourself being affected by any of the great Mental Waves of feeling or emotion sweeping over the public mind, and which have a tendency to "stampede" people into adopting certain ideas, or of following certain leaders. In such case the assertion of the "I" within you will dissipate the influence around you, and you will find yourself standing in a center of Peace surrounded on all sides by the ocean of mental tumult and agitation which is sweeping over or circling around the place. In the same way you will be able to neutralize the unpleasant mental atmospheres of places, localities, houses, etc., and render yourself positive to and immune from the same. n short, we have given you here a recipe that may be used in any and every instance of the employment of Mental Influence. It may sound simple to you, but a little use of it will make you deem it the most important bit of practical knowledge you may possess.

Made in the USA
Middletown, DE
03 February 2018